POLICING AND JUSTICE

Dirk Flint

W

FRANKLIN WATTS
LONDON • SYDNEY

First published in 2011 by
Franklin Watts
338 Euston Road
London NW1 3BH

Franklin Watts Australia
Level 17/207 Kent Street
Sydney NSW 2000

Series editor: Jeremy Smith
Editor: Julia Bird
Design: sprout.uk.com
Artworks: sprout.uk.com
Picture researcher: Diana Morris

A CIP catalogue record for this book is available
from the British Library.

ISBN 978 0 7496 9587 3

Dewey classification: 363.2'3

Printed in China

Franklin Watts is a division of Hachette Children's
Books, an Hachette UK company.
www.hachette.co.uk

Picture credits: AFP/Getty Images: 14.
AP/PAI: 30. Anthony Baggett/istockphoto: 8t.
Graham Barclay/Bloomberg/Getty Images: 25b.
Tamara Beckwith/Rex Features: 36. Brendan Beirne/
Rex Features: 12. Nicholas Campbell/istockphoto:
40b. Peter Casolino/Alamy: 13tl. Ron Chapple/Getty
Images: 28. CNN/Getty Images: 18.Stephen
Coburn/Shutterstock: 13tr. Jeff Damone/Alamy: front
cover c. Fortean/Topfoto: 10. Foto 24/Alamy: 31.
Richard Gardner/Rex Features: 32. Anat Givon/AP/
PAI: 22. Stan Honda/AFP/Getty Images: 40t. KPA/
Zuma/Rex Features: 16. Jonathan Larsen/
istockphoto: 24. Lehtikuva Oy/Rex Features: 33t.
Brennan Linsley/AP/PAI: 37. Andrew Medicini/AP/
PAI: 38. Gianni Muratore/Alamy: 33b.
PA/Topham: 23. Tim Pannell/Corbis: 25t.
Photos 12/Alamy: 20. Picturepoint/Topham: 29.
Oliver Pirard/Rex Features: 35. Joe Raedle/Getty
Images: 26. Ren Photo/istockphoto: 34, posed by
model. Rex Features: 41. Stefan Rousseau/PA/PAI:
21. Gina Sanders/Shutterstock: front cover b, 5.
Shutterstock: front cover t. Sipa Press/Rex Features:
11, 15. Paula Solloway/Photofusion: 39. Times
Newspapers/Rex Features: 19. Patrick Urban/Alamy:
8b. Rui Viera/PA/PAI: 9. A.T.Willet/Alamy: 27. Steve
Yeater/AP/PAI: 17.

CONTENTS

WHAT IS CRIMINAL JUSTICE?

When a police officer makes an arrest for a crime, it is just the first step in a long legal process that involves lawyers, judges, prison staff and probation officers. The idea behind this system, known as 'criminal justice', is that crimes should be suitably and fairly punished.

Crime and punishment

Like most people, if you were the victim of a crime, you would expect the state to do something about it. In most countries, this involves a police investigation and arrest, followed by a trial in a court. Anyone found guilty of crime is punished. Steps are also taken to prevent further crimes, and to help you as the victim. Criminal justice works on the principle that punishing criminals reduces crime, and makes everyone else safer. The word 'justice' also suggests that everyone involved in the arrest and trial should aim to be fair. In practice, however, this can be hard to achieve. There are famous cases where innocent people have been put in prison or even executed.

▶ *The statue of Lady Justice stands on the dome above the Central Criminal Court in London. She holds the scales of justice in her left hand to weigh up the evidence, and a raised sword in her right hand to punish offenders.*

▼ *Police officers carry out a wide range of duties to keep people in the community safe, including directing traffic.*

What part do the police play?

The police are mainly involved at the start of the criminal justice process. They arrest suspects and collect evidence that can later be used in court. In TV shows, we see them endlessly chasing down hardened criminals in speeding cars. While some detectives do carry out this work, they also have to do a lot of paperwork to make sure that any evidence they gather will stand up in court. But keeping people safe isn't just about catching criminals. Most police officers carry out a much wider range of jobs, from traffic duties to policing football matches.

How much crime is there?

In 2009–10 there were over four million crimes committed in England and Wales. That can seem like a lot for 140,000 officers to tackle. However, it is important to remember that most crimes are comparatively petty, such as vandalism or drunkenness, and many cases never go to court. By comparison, in the United States in 2008 law enforcement officers made over 14 million arrests: of these criminal acts, around 600,000 were violent crimes.

ON TARGET

The police are bound by the law like everyone else. As part of their training, police officers learn what powers they have when trying to catch or question a suspect. It takes skill to catch an escaping criminal without needing to use force, especially if the suspect is armed. New weapons may cut down on the number of confrontations: flying robots armed with powerful strobes may soon be used to stop fleeing criminals in their tracks by making them dizzy!

▼ In the future, the police may use robot probes like the flying AirRobot to help them track or catch criminals. An electric engine allows the robot to fly or hover silently overhead, while thermal-imaging cameras can spot hidden suspects by sensing their body heat.

ROUGH JUSTICE

Criminal justice is as old as crime. In ancient times, there were many harsh laws and brutal punishments even for petty crimes, such as stealing a loaf of bread. Over time criminal justice has undoubtedly become less harsh in most countries, with more focus on issues such as human rights and victim support.

How did it all start?

Most people obey most laws willingly, as long as the laws are fair. To maintain order, most ancient communities made up their own rules about how their members should behave. Justice in those days was rough and ready, however, and the laws were usually enforced by the personal bodyguards of rulers and warlords. Punishments were often extreme, such as hangings, beheadings or brandings with a hot iron.

A changing world

In medieval times, (from the 5th to the 15th century) there were no official police forces. Instead, communities relied on their members to punish wrongdoing. The first real police forces appeared in the 19th century, such as the London

▲ Today there are strict laws about how the police treat suspects. But in medieval times, suspects were often cruelly tortured to force them to confess.

BUSTED!

Police forces constantly have to adapt to keep up with criminals. The spread of computers and the Internet, for example, has led to a new kind of crime: cybercrime. In response to this, in 2008, the UK Metropolitan Police set up a National E-Crime Unit. In April 2009 it launched its first successful raid, on a gang using a computer virus to hack into bank accounts, and in December 2009 it shut down over 1,200 scam websites targeting Christmas shoppers with fake designer goods.

Metropolitan Police (1829) and the Boston Police Department (1838). Modern law courts and prisons also developed around this time. The US Bill of Rights first banned the use of 'cruel and unusual punishment' on people held by the police in 1791. Today, criminal justice systems are still evolving. There is a lot more focus now on issues such as youth justice, human rights and the rights of victims.

A long way to go?

Campaigners believe there is still a lot to be done to make policing more effective and to create a court system that treats people from all backgrounds fairly. But it is often a long, uphill battle to reform the legal system. In France, some serious crimes are investigated by a *juge d'instruction* or magistrate, who investigates the crime and recommends whether a suspect should be prosecuted or cleared. However, this legal system can be flawed. In 2000, 13 people were wrongly imprisoned after an investigation by a young, inexperienced magistrate in the town of Boulogne. Ten years on, French President Nicolas Sarkozy's plans to abolish these *juges d'instruction* are being fiercely resisted by lawyers who believe it will make the investigations less impartial.

▲ *In the past, individual rulers made the laws and decided who was guilty and who was innocent. Today, the laws in most countries are created by a parliament, such as the European Parliament shown above, while the courts are responsible for judging whether the laws have been broken and for punishing offenders.*

ON TARGET

In recent years, many European countries have reformed their criminal laws. Many have replaced light prison sentences with fines or community service. Other new laws are designed to tackle new forms of crime, simplify older laws or make policing more effective. Which laws do you consider might need updating or changing to be effective in today's world?

ENFORCING THE LAW

At the sharp end of the criminal justice system are the police officers we see every day on the street and the detectives who investigate crimes. However, the state also relies on many other groups and individuals to enforce the law, including social workers, safety inspectors, tax officials, customs officers and private security guards, as well as charities such as the NSPCC or RSPCA.

National vs local

Most police services combine local and national forces. In the United States, the sheriff provides services for each county. Towns and cities have their own police chief, while state troopers have authority over the whole state. This is the same in Australia. In the United Kingdom, the police service is divided into regions. In theory, a national police force is more efficient as resources are not duplicated and officers are all trained in the one system. For example, in Germany the Federal Police Academy in Lübeck oversees all training and coordinates the five training centres around the country. However, there is always a danger that the government can use its control of the police to keep itself in office.

Community policing

The last 30 years has seen a move towards community policing, based on the idea that crimes are more likely to be solved when the police have the support of local people. Community police officers work closely with a particular neighbourhood and are more likely to walk the beat or ride a bicycle than drive a patrol car. Community policing gives communities a chance to tell the police what they want from them. It also makes people feel safer and less worried about crime. On the other hand, there can be fewer officers in cars ready to respond quickly to crimes.

▼ *The Australian Federal Police (AFP) is a national police force that serves the whole of Australia. Here, police officers in New South Wales are keeping an eye on the crowds at Bondi Beach, Sydney.*

▲ Police officers can tackle crime more effectively if they have the support of the local community. Here an officer talks to teenagers in an inner city housing project in New Haven, Connecticut, USA.

▲ Neighbourhood Watch schemes encourage members to report suspicious activity to the police. They also promote better home security and can reduce people's fear of crime.

DIY crimebusters

Neighbourhood Watch schemes ask ordinary people at home to keep their eyes and ears open for anything unusual going on in their neighbourhoods. Some communities even organise patrols at certain times during the day or night. But some experts argue that crime prevention should be left to the professionals. It can be very dangerous to confront criminals. In January 2010 in London an Indian national, Sukhwinder Singh, was stabbed to death after giving chase to two men who had stolen a woman's handbag.

BUSTED!

In October 2007, a Neighbourhood Watch scheme in Winona, Minnesota, USA led to a major drug bust after residents wrote down car licence plate numbers and reported suspicious activity to police. Following the tip-off, officers tracked down and charged 14 suspects.

DEALING WITH SERIOUS CRIMES

More serious crimes, such as large-scale fraud, murder and terrorism, are usually dealt with by national and international crime-fighting agencies such as the Federal Bureau of Investigation (FBI) in the United States and the Serious Organised Crime Agency (SOCA) in the UK. When criminal gangs are based in one country and operating in many others, international police co-operation is needed to bring them to justice.

The growth of international crime

In the last ten years, organised crime has become a vast and truly international business, from drug running and illegal arms deals to trafficking in human beings. International policing organisations such as Europol and Interpol help national police forces to work together by storing and sharing information on criminals worldwide. For example, before the FIFA World Cup in South Africa in 2010, Interpol organised a meeting of officers from all 32 participating nations to discuss security at the event.

ON TARGET

Interpol's global police communications system, known as I-24/7, allows police forces to search and cross-check data in a matter of seconds, whether tracking down suspected terrorists, fugitives, fingerprints, stolen cars or even stolen works of art. In 2009, the database got 70,000 positive hits from national police forces looking for information on a suspect.

◀ Greek police officers escort Australian drug baron Tony Mokbel into court in October 2007. Mokbel fled to Greece when on trial in Australia, but international police co-operation led to his re-capture.

Federal police forces

The criminal justice system usually relies on a national police force to investigate more complex cases such as cybercrime, drug trafficking, organised crime, money laundering and people smuggling, as local forces do not have the resources or specialists needed on such cases. However, national police officers often have to work closely with local police organisations so that they can benefit from knowledge of regular street police who know the neighbourhood.

International justice

Many countries have treaties with each other so that criminals who have fled abroad can be forced to return to face prosecution (known as extradition). However, countries may refuse to extradite suspected criminals, especially if they are likely to face the death penalty or be tortured. Sometimes they hold their own trials instead. In 2002, an International Criminal Court was set up in the Hague, the Netherlands to deal with war crimes and crimes against humanity that national courts will not or cannot investigate.

ON TARGET

In 1983, the US Marshals Service set up the 15 Most Wanted Fugitives Program to publicise the names of some of the country's most dangerous criminals who are on the run from the police. These include murderers, gang bosses or drug barons. In 2007, US Marshals captured over 36,000 fugitives from the law. The US Marshals unit also guards courts, transports prisoners and protects federal witnesses.

▼ The International Criminal Court (ICC) in the Hague, the Netherlands was set up in 2002 to prosecute individuals for war crimes and genocide.

OFFICERS OF THE LAW

The various local and national police forces play a crucial role in the criminal justice system, as they are responsible for investigating crimes, making arrests and collecting evidence. In a democratic country, people should be able to expect the police to treat everyone fairly and to operate within the law.

Closed ranks

The tough nature of police work means that police officers can become very loyal and close-knit. As a result, women, homosexuals and people from ethnic minorities can find the police force a tough environment to work in. There have been many high profile initiatives to address this. For example, in 1999 police forces in England and Wales were set recruitment targets for black and Asian officers that reflected their local community, and since then the number of such officers has doubled. Female police officers, however, still only make up around 25% of the police force in the UK, while only around 12% of US police officers are women.

Challenges

Dealing with criminals on a daily basis is not for the faint-hearted, and young police officers are often shocked by the grim reality of life on the streets. Officers can also find the mountains of paperwork and the often slow legal process very frustrating. As a result, some become cynical about the justice system and focus more on making sure they get a conviction than treating people fairly. While similar problems do exist in other professions, the difference is that police attitudes have a big effect on the criminal justice process. In many incidents, it is up to individual officers on the spot to decide how to handle a situation.

▼ Female officers in the Kashmir Police Services take part in a parade in Srinagar, Kashmir, India. Around the world, female officers have shown they can handle dangerous situations.

ON TARGET

Many police forces have initiated schemes in an attempt to counter prejudices among their officers. In 2000, the Metropolitan Police Authority (MPA) was set up to make sure that London's police are accountable for the services they provide to people in the capital. It has led to initiatives to improve relations between the police and minority groups, including a scheme whereby gay people can report crimes without having to contact the police directly.

High standards

Good policing can make life safer and more secure for everyone, which is why there are often calls by the public for more police officers on the streets. A good officer can earn the trust and respect of the local community, which will also make their job a lot easier. But an officer who misuses their power or discriminates against certain groups undermines both their own unit and the whole criminal justice system. In a democracy, we should expect only the highest standards from the police.

Awards

Police forces around the world recognise officers who have performed particularly brave or heroic acts with awards and decorations. In the UK, outstanding police officers can be awarded a National Police Bravery Award, while every officer who is killed in the line of duty is added to a Roll of Honour. In the US, each regional police force decorates its own outstanding officers with such prestigious awards as the Medal of Valor or the Police Purple Heart.

▶ The Governor of California, ex-actor Arnold Schwarzenegger, presents a police officer with a Medal of Valor. The award is given to those officers who have performed above and beyond the call of duty.

CASE STUDY:
RACISM IN THE POLICE

Racism can be a problem in police forces around the world. In practice, this means that some officers decide to stop or arrest a suspect because of their colour or ethnic background rather than because they were doing anything suspicious. In extreme cases, police units have deliberately attacked people from minority groups.

Rodney King

In March 1991, officers from the Los Angeles Police Department were caught on videotape repeatedly hitting an African-American suspect, Rodney King, with their batons. When a court later found the police officers not guilty of the attack, anger in the African-American community of Los Angeles boiled over, resulting in a six-day riot that claimed 53 lives and caused $1 billion (UK £620 million) worth of damage to property. The beating, the acquittals and the riot that followed put the spotlight on racism and police brutality, and the lack of fairness in the US criminal justice system.

Loss of trust

Racist behaviour among the police can soon lead to a loss of trust among the community. As a result, it becomes very hard for the police to work effectively, as they can no longer rely on local people to come forward as witnesses. In some neighbourhoods, things can get so bad that they become 'no-go' areas for the police. In October 2005,

▼ On 3 March 1991, Rodney King was pulled over by Los Angeles police officers after a high-speed chase. A witness filmed the scene from his apartment. His video showed the officers beating and kicking King. It shocked viewers when it was shown on TV.

MAR. 3 1991

two African-French youths were electrocuted as they fled the police in a Parisian suburb. Their deaths sparked nearly three weeks of rioting in 274 towns throughout France. These were partly a protest against heavy-handed policing, and during the riots eight police officers were suspended for beating up someone they had arrested.

The MacPherson Report

Even when police officers are not directly involved, racist attacks can expose police racism. On 22 April 1993, 18-year-old Stephen Lawrence was stabbed to death in an unprovoked attack by a gang of white youths in southeast London. During the police investigation, five suspects were arrested but never convicted. Stephen's parents were angry at the way the police had handled the case and campaigned tirelessly for the case to be looked at again. Due to their determination, a public inquiry was set up

in 1997. Two years later, the MacPherson report revealed widespread racism within the Metropolitan Police, from the abuse of black police officers to a failure to treat racial crimes seriously. The report contained 70 recommendations designed to improve police accountability, among other aims.

► *Doreen and Neville Lawrence, parents of murdered black teenager Stephen Lawrence. Their efforts brought institutional police racism to public attention.*

ON TARGET

Many police forces are taking steps to address racism, such as setting up minority police associations, increasing anti-racism training and hiring more officers from minority groups. Other forces have introduced Multicultural Liaison Units or trained officers in specific languages and cultures to encourage better relations with ethnic communities.

GUARDING THE GUARDIANS

When one group of police officers investigates another police unit, they are put in a difficult position. Bound by the police code of honour, some may find it hard to evaluate fellow officers fairly. Though in the past there have been some notorious cover-ups, there have also been many high-profile cases where police investigators have revealed corruption or other wrongdoings within their own force.

The use of force

Police forces are especially criticised for using unnecessary force in making arrests and detaining suspects. In 1979, New Zealand teacher Blair Peach was killed by a police officer during an anti-racism rally in London, but crucial evidence relating to the investigation was covered up. The Metropolitan Police only admitted responsibility for Peach's death in a report in 2010. In Australia, a Royal Commission was set up in 1987 to investigate the high numbers of Aborigines who died while in police custody. There are also concerns about the number of deaths caused by high speed police pursuits. In August 2009 eight people died after three US teenagers trying to outrun the police hit a family car.

BUSTED!

In the early 1970s, detective Frank Serpico bravely helped to blow the lid off corruption in the New York Police Department. The scandal led to a massive reform and a number of convictions. 'Whistleblowers' often risk losing their job or being bullied by other staff members, but in Ireland a new charter is now being introduced that will give them complete protection if they uncover corruption.

▶ In the 1973 movie, Serpico, Al Pacino played Frank Serpico, the detective who blew the whistle on corruption in the New York Police Department.

Police investigations

Police services commonly include units for investigating crimes committed by the police themselves. In the United States, around 190 FBI special agents tackle such cases. In the UK officers from other parts of the force are often called in to investigate. In the 1970s, a team from outside London, the so-called 'Operation Countrymen', revealed an extensive and tangled web of corruption in the Metropolitan Police force. Such inquiries are needed to weed out 'bad apples' such as corrupt or violent officers. More importantly, they can also lead to new policies that can change attitudes throughout the force.

Making a complaint

Many countries have set up complaints organisations that are independent of the police force. In the United States, cities such as Washington DC and San Francisco have their own office of complaints staffed only by people who have never been members of the local police force. In the UK, complaints are made to the Independent Police Complaints Commission (IPCC). By contrast in France, where there is no such organisation, a high number of complaints are closed without a trial, while few officers are ever convicted.

ON TARGET

Almost all police forces routinely carry firearms, with a few notable exceptions such as the UK, Norway and New Zealand. Inevitably, both criminals and innocent bystanders can get injured or killed by police officers. Such shootings are very controversial, so in Canada, a Special Investigations Unit, independent of the police, has been set up to investigate police shootings that result in a serious injury or death.

▶ Nick Hardwick, then Chairman of the IPCC, oversees a press conference following the IPCC's report into the death of Jean Charles de Menezes. De Menezes was shot dead by police who mistook him for a suicide bomber on London's Underground in 2005 (see p.36).

CASE STUDY: REFORMING THE POLICE

When many people have lost faith in their police force, sometimes the only option is radical reform or a mass purge of corrupt officers.

The ICAC

In the 1970s, corruption was a huge problem in the Hong Kong Police, so the Independent Commission Against Corruption (ICAC) was created to clean up the force. After a series of investigations, in 1978 some 119 officers were sacked and another further 24 officers were held on conspiracy charges. Thanks to the ICAC, 30 years later the Hong Kong Police still has a reputation as one of the least corrupt forces in the world.

▼ *Officers from the Hong Kong Police guard a court room. Today the force has a good reputation thanks to the Independent Commission Against Corruption, which ruthlessly rooted out corruption during the 1970s.*

The RUC

The Royal Ulster Constabulary (RUC) was the state police force in Northern Ireland. It was also a peacekeeping force alongside the British Army, and was often involved in violent clashes with the Irish Republican Army and other nationalist groups who wanted the end of British rule in Northern Ireland. The Stephens Inquiry in 2003 revealed that RUC officers were involved in the murders of several nationalists. No wonder then that reform of the RUC was an important part of the Good Friday Agreement in 1998 that brought peace to Northern Ireland.

◄ Officers from the new Police Service of Northern Ireland (PSNI) on parade. The PSNI was created to replace the old Royal Ulster Constabulary.

A new police force

The Patten Report in 1999 led to the creation of the new Police Service of Northern Ireland (PSNI) based on human rights and community policing. This is now said by some to be the most accountable police force in the world. The force was given a new badge and uniform, and more significantly, it now recruits half of its officers from a Catholic background. Traditionally the RUC had strong Protestant connections, and there were many complaints of RUC mistreatment of Catholic suspects and prisoners.

ON TARGET

Following a series of brutal crimes by police officers, in 2010 Russian President Dmitry Medvedev sacked 17 top police generals and introduced tougher punishments for police officers found guilty of committing crimes. The Russian government also asked its citizens to comment on proposals for police reform after releasing the proposals online.

THE CRIMINAL JUSTICE SYSTEM

When it comes to tackling crime, police officers work alongside other agencies such as prosecutors, courts, the probation service and youth offending services. But there is more to the criminal justice system than handing out punishments to criminals. While its ultimate aim is usually to reduce crime and make people safer, it has to be seen to deal with everyone fairly and equally, while protecting individual rights.

What system?

When we talk about the criminal justice 'system', it is easy to think of it as carefully planned and coordinated. In reality, most systems have grown up over hundreds of years and contain some parts that are very old, such as jury trials, and others that are new, such as victim support. Police services, law courts and probation officers all have their own goals and priorities that often clash with other parts of the system. However, they are all very closely linked, and a reform in one part of the system can have a major effect on other elements.

How it works

There are four main parts to the criminal justice system:

- law enforcement and detention

- trial and sentencing

- punishment

- help for the victim.

▼ *In the United States, as in many other countries, most trials take place in district courts. The Supreme Court, pictured below, acts as a high court and has the final say on disputes, appeals and interpreting the meaning of laws.*

◀ In the US and UK court systems, trial lawyers argue on behalf of their clients in an attempt to persuade the jury that they are innocent of the charges brought against them.

The trial

We have already looked at the role played by the police in enforcing the law. The courts are responsible for trials and sentencing decisions. The entire trial process is lengthy and can be fraught with problems, but justice must be seen to be done within the courtroom. Any prejudice on the part of the lawyers, the judge, or, if applicable, jury members threatens to destroy the court's credibility.

Punishment

Those convicted of a crime are punished according to the crime committed. Sentences can vary widely from country to country, but problems such as overcrowded prisons have led to an increase in alternatives such as fines and community sentences. There is also greater recognition in many countries that young offenders need to be dealt with differently from adults, and that victims should play an important part in the justice system.

▶ Prison populations have risen dramatically in the last 20 years in countries such as the UK and the United States. This is not because more crimes are being committed, but because sentences have become harsher.

ON TARGET

Courts are now using hi-tech gadgets to improve trials. In Malaysia, where Malay, Chinese, Tamil, Javanese, and English are all commonly spoken, a new system was used in court for the first time in 2009. After an interpreter types out what a witness is saying, the translation is then flashed onto a screen so that everyone in court can immediately understand what has just been said.

ARREST AND DETENTION

If the police tried to enforce every law all of the time, life would soon come to a grinding halt – there are just too many laws. So a good officer will know when to make an arrest (and when not to), and how to do it in a way that protects the public. Once arrested, suspects are taken to a police station where they are detained to ensure that they appear before a court to answer charges, and to ensure that crimes are properly investigated.

When to arrest?

When called to an incident, a police officer may have to act as judge and jury, for example when there is a fight between a husband and wife. In some cases, he may decide to arrest a violent husband, in others, he may simply caution him. This is known as discretion. When an arrest is made, the suspect must be told the reason for it.

▼ A police officer makes an arrest in Miami, USA. A reason for the arrest must be given at the time of the arrest for it to be legal.

Custody

In most countries, there are laws about how long a suspect can be held without being charged. In the UK for example, unless you are suspected of terrorist activities, you cannot be held for longer than 36 hours. An officer must also have reasonable suspicion that the suspect is involved in a crime or intending to carry one out. Once in police custody, the suspect has the right to legal advice. Though the police have the right to ask questions, except in a few circumstances, the suspect does not have to

▲ *Police interrogations are usually carried out in small, soundproof rooms with just a few chairs and a desk, and nothing on the walls.*

provide an answer (this is known as the right to remain silent). Once the suspect is brought to a station, he or she must be charged with a crime within a certain amount of time. For most crimes, this is a few hours.

The investigation

While a suspect is in custody, the police work fast to investigate the crime scene, gather evidence and interview witnesses so that they can build a case. On TV, interrogations usually occur in the police station, but in real life they also take place at the crime scene before the suspect is arrested. One of the best pieces of evidence is when a suspect says something that can be proven to be a lie. Physical evidence such as fingerprints, murder weapons and hairs can also help the police to make a case. Then the investigating officer writes a detailed report which is sent to the prosecutor, who decides whether the case should be tried in court. If the prosecutor decides that the case against the suspect is strong enough, the suspect will be formally charged with the crime and tried. If the case is not strong enough, the suspect is released without charges.

ON TARGET

A confession from a suspect is about the best evidence you can have, but confessions are not always reliable. Today, officers use a variety of tricks to get a confession from a suspect, such as pretending that another suspect has already pointed the finger at them. Critics argue that such tactics are illegal. It can get much worse: during the 1970s and 80s, the UK West Midlands Serious Crime Squad terrorised suspects by suffocating them with plastic bags until they passed out. The squad was disbanded in 1989 and 30 convictions were later overturned. In 1997, the Criminal Cases Review Commission was set up to review similar miscarriages of justice.

YOUTH JUSTICE

In the early 1800s, small children were executed for picking someone's pocket. Slowly, the laws in many countries recognised that children should be treated differently to adults. While young offenders are still sent to prison, education programmes and counselling can help children and teenagers move away from doing things which might get them or their friends into trouble with the law.

Changing views

Today, it is understood that children who are jailed often come from a background of neglect or have mental health issues, and need support rather than punishment. As a result, programmes providing employment or counselling are often more successful at cutting crime than simply punishing the offender. In the UK almost 75% of young people who are put in custody later carry out another crime.

ON TARGET

In some US states, volunteer mentors from groups such as Mentoring Today help young offenders to steer clear of crime. For a child with a troubled background, knowing that someone is looking out for them can make a big difference. Abdul Mujahid Rashid, 18, from Washington DC, explains how a mentor can make all the difference: 'When I got out [from prison], they helped me get a job, helped me get into school, helped my mother when she had no food.'

Bootcamp

Despite this, rising levels of youth crime have led to calls for tougher sentences for young offenders. In the Netherlands, a recent programme has seen hardened young criminals sent to 'bootcamps' with very strict rules.

◄ In most countries, a teenager can be convicted of a crime. Most child experts agree that children and teenagers who commit offences need to be treated rather than punished.

► Young offenders in this Belgium youth prison are encouraged to do activities such as sports and gardening. Working in a team is thought to help them learn how to be more responsible for their actions.

ASBOs

In the UK, children as young as 10 can be served with anti-social behaviour orders (ASBOs). These are often used to prevent minor offences such as graffiti, vandalism or aggressive behaviour. For example, a teenager found guilty of violent drunken behaviour might be banned from pubs and off-licences. However, critics argue that some children think getting an ASBO simply gives them more 'street cred'. There is also a lot of controversy over the age at which a child is responsible for his or her actions. In France, plans to put children as young as 12 in custody caused social workers to go on strike in protest in 2008.

New approaches

In Northern Ireland, one pilot scheme is getting young offenders to face their victims to help them recognise the harm they have done and ensure that they work hard to make up for it. In Florida, USA another scheme has been launched that helps parents spot if their children have joined a criminal gang so that they can intervene before their son or daughter gets into trouble with the law.

FACT FILE

Criminal responsibility

The age you can be put in prison for committing a crime differs from country to country. This stems from differing views about what age a young person fully understands that they know they're doing wrong when they commit a crime. This is known as criminal responsibility.

Age	Country
7	India, South Africa, Thailand, Pakistan
8	Scotland, Kenya, Indonesia
9	Ethiopia, Iran
10	England, Wales, Ukraine, Nepal
11	Turkey
12	Ireland, South Korea, Netherlands, Uganda, Canada
13	France, Algeria, Poland
14	Germany, China, Italy, Japan, Russia, Vietnam
16	Argentina

(The age of criminal responsibility in the US varies between 6 and 12, depending on the state.)

VICTIMS' RIGHTS

In the past, victims of crime were chiefly regarded as useful witnesses and were often made to feel little more than pieces of evidence. But many countries are now placing victims at the heart of the criminal justice process and have adopted a Victims' Charter. This informs victims of crime what sort of service they can expect from law enforcement agencies when they report a crime.

Victim organisations

In some countries, such as Japan, every prosecutor's office has its own Victim Support Officer, while in others independent organisations assist victims of crime. They can help answer questions the victims might have, as well as accompanying them to the courthouse. Some victim's groups have also managed to bring about important changes in the law, such as 'Megan's Law' in the United States, which requires law enforcement agencies to notify the public when a sex offender is released into their community, along with details about his or her crimes.

Protecting victims

Victims are often key witnesses, but it can be very painful for victims to have to give evidence in court and relive their ordeal, especially in cases such as kidnapping or rape. Today, screens in court allow victims or offenders to make statements via video link rather than having to face one another in court. In some cases, the victim is in a separate location. In others, the offender appears in court via a live video link from prison.

▼ *In June 2010, jailed Sicilian mafia boss Toto Riina appeared in court via a link from Milan's high-security Opera prison, where he is serving multiple life sentences for murder.*

▲ *Here victims meet with their attacker. In other mediation schemes, victims and offenders do not meet directly but communicate via another person.*

Meeting your attacker

Since the 1990s, countries such as China, Germany, Sweden and Denmark have experimented with mediation schemes in which victims get a chance to meet their offender. Surveys have shown that such meetings often help victims feel less angry and afraid. Meeting the victim can help the offender, too. It gives them a chance to understand the consequences of what they have done, and to offer an apology. As a result, it can make them feel more like a person, rather than a criminal, and may deter them from committing further crimes. Critics point out that mediation, though useful, can be used as a tool by lawyers to help their clients get a lighter sentence.

ON TARGET

Some victim support groups focus on young victims of crime, who may find it hard to speak out about how a crime has affected them. As one member of a support group based in Norfolk in England said: 'Being a victim of crime affects you both physically and mentally. After I was attacked, Victim Support helped me to repair my self-confidence and get my life back on track while the doctors sorted out my physical problems.'

THE FUTURE

No criminal justice system is perfect. Prisons are expensive to run and increasingly overcrowded. Some innocent people are sent to prison and police officers can be found guilty of abusing their power. But in many countries, governments and independent organisations continue to work hard to provide services that are fair and effective. So what can we expect in the future?

Catching up with criminals

Crime is always changing and criminal justice systems are constantly playing catch-up. The population is getting older in most developed countries, so there may be a need for greater protection for the elderly – though it could also mean that there are more elderly people at home to report suspicious activities or steer children away from crime. There may also be a shift towards more trials involving complex crimes such as fraud being held without juries. In the UK, more specialist courts are being set up to deal with crimes linked to drugs, violence in the home or mental health.

▶ *Most people feel safer when they see police officers out on the beat. But other tactics are better at detecting and preventing crime. Which is more important?*

▼ *CCTV cameras help to record crimes and can deter criminals from committing crimes in the first place. In the future, face recognition technology could allow the police to pinpoint a suspect's exact location at any given time.*

New technology

Developments in surveillance and DNA analysis will help crimefighters everywhere, while increasingly sophisticated intelligence databases may in future be used by the general public as well as police officers. Technology could also help the work of organisations like the Criminal Assets Bureau in Ireland, which seizes money, houses and cars from convicted criminals, especially those in organised gangs. However, the spread of new technology will also lead to new forms of crime – just as mobile phones led to the rise of bullying text messages and the development of the Internet has led to the quickfire spread of cybercrime.

FACT FILE

Sadly, most big changes in policing or the criminal justice system are brought about by scandals or devastating events like the terrorist attacks on New York (see p.36). On 1 April 2009, newspaper vendor Ian Tomlinson collapsed and died on his way home from work during protests in London. Amateur video footage showed him being struck by a police baton. In response, the Chief Inspector of Constabulary, Denis O'Connor, published a 150-page report in November 2009 that aims to bring sweeping reforms to how the police deal with similar protests.

Prison vs welfare

Undoubtedly the battle will continue between those who would like to see more people behind bars and those who believe education and training programmes are the best way to cut crime. One major recent study found that a variety of individual counselling, interpersonal skills training and other behavioural programmes in the United States were shown to reduce reoffending by 40%. In the future, more schemes that deal with young offenders may prove a valuable tool in tackling crime. In the meantime, it is worth bearing in mind that newspapers, TV and the Internet always focus on the worst crimes, and most people's chances of being caught up in serious crime are relatively slim.

▶ *When newspaper seller Ian Tomlinson (here sitting on the ground) died after being knocked to the ground by a police officer on 21 April 2009, there was a huge public outcry. His death led to new guidelines on the use of force by police officers in the UK.*

GLOSSARY

Acquittal Being declared not guilty of a particular crime.

Appeal Court The higher court, such as the Court of Appeal, to which cases are sent when either the defence or prosecution wish to challenge the result made in court.

Arms Guns such as handguns, shotguns or rifles.

Arrest Lawful detention by a police officer.

Bail Release from custody, usually with some conditions that will guarantee someone's appearance at court.

Caution A formal warning from the police, usually given to people who admit they are guilty of minor first-time offences such as theft.

Community policing A way of policing whereby the police and the local community work together to solve and prevent crime.

Community sentence When an offender is not sent to prison, but sentenced to serve in the community – usually unpaid work, job training, counselling (or all three).

Criminal justice system The system of enforcing the law and preventing crime, combining many different organisations such as the police, the courts and the prison service.

Criminal responsibility For someone to be responsible for carrying out a crime, they must understand what they are doing and that it is wrong. In most countries, people with severe mental health problems and children under a certain age cannot be held criminally responsible for their actions.

Curfew Similar to house arrest – people must stay indoors, usually at their home, during certain hours.

Custody Held or locked-up by the police.

Cybercrime When the Internet or computer networks are used to commit crimes such as stealing a person's identity, selling illegal goods or stalking victims.

Defendant The person standing trial.

Discrimination To treat someone differently based purely on attributes such as his or her age, race, sex, or religion.

Electronic tag A device used to track a criminal when they are under curfew or on bail.

Extradition When a criminal suspect held by one government is handed over to another government for trial.

Federal An organisation or officer with authority over the whole country rather than just one region or state.

Forensics Scientific tests used to investigate crimes.

Fraud The crime of obtaining money or some other benefit by deliberately deceiving or lying to others.

Human rights Basic rights and freedoms belonging to all humans, such as the right to life and the right to be treated the same as any other person by the law.

Jury A group of people sworn to try a case and reach a verdict according to the evidence given in court.

Mediation When a third party negotiates between the victim of a crime and the offender.

Mentor Someone who acts as a trusted guide or advisor.

Miscarriage of justice When someone has been sentenced for a crime they didn't commit.

Money laundering Hiding the source of illegally-made money by investing in legal businesses or moving it from one bank account to another.

Offender Someone who has been convicted of a crime.

Prosecutor A government lawyer who decides whether to charge a person with a crime and tries to prove in court that the person is guilty.

Rehabilitation Helping offenders to find a useful place in society.

Statutory sentence A sentence that is fixed by law, such as a minimum sentence for murder.

Trafficking Smuggling illegal goods, especially drugs.

FURTHER INFORMATION

Books

Sean Sheehan, *A Young Citizen's Guide to the Criminal Justice System*, Wayland, 2011

Christopher Riches, *Britain: The Facts: Law and Order*, Franklin Watts, 2008

Websites

www.justice.gov/dea/index.htm
Home page of the US Department of Justice, with lots of news about recent cases, plus a report on Guantanamo Bay.

www.direct.gov.uk/en/YoungPeople/CrimeAndJustice/index.htm
Government website explaining how the criminal justice system works in the UK.

www.judiciary.state.nj.us/kids/index.htm
Website explaining how courts work in the US, in particular in the state of New Jersey.

www1.curriculum.edu.au/ddunits/guide/guide.htm
Useful information on laws and rights in Australia.

encyclopedia.kids.net.au/page/cr/Criminal_justice
General information on criminal justice systems around the world.

www.un.org/cyberschoolbus/humanrights/index.asp
United Nations site explaining human rights.

www.hht.net.au/museums/justice_and_police_museum
Website of Sydney's historical Justice and Police Museum, with a large collection of great archive photographs.

www.interpol.int/public/icpo/default.asp
All about INTERPOL, the world's largest international police organisation.

news.bbc.co.uk/2/hi/special_report/1999/02/99/stephen_lawrence/285357.stm
The BBC report on the Stephen Lawrence murder investigation.

www.psni.police.uk
Find out more about the Police Service of Northern Ireland.

www.fearless.org
A website that allows you to give information about crime online, part of the charity Crimestoppers.

www.soca.gov.uk
Website of the UK's Serious Organised Crime Agency.

www.fbi.gov
Website of the US Federal Bureau of Investigation.

Note to parents and teachers: every effort has been made by the Publishers to ensure that these websites are suitable for children, that they are of the highest educational value, and that they contain no inappropriate or offensive material. However, because of the nature of the Internet, it is impossible to guarantee that the contents of these sites will not be altered. We strongly advise that Internet access is supervised by a responsible adult.

INDEX

SERIES CONTENTS

Cybercrime Hacking • Case study: Gary McKinnon • Phishing • Cyberbullying • Cyberstalking • Virus attacks • Malware • Social networking sites • Fraudulent websites • Denial-of-service attacks • Identity theft • Case study: Pirate Bay • Cyberterrorism • Cyberwars • Case study: Cyberwars in Eastern Europe • Cybersecurity

Drug crime Worldwide drug problem • Which drugs are illegal? • Who are the criminals? • The flow of drugs • The cost of drugs • Tackling the traffickers • Smuggling and mules • Below the waves • Stop and search • Global drug watch • Surveillance • Operation Junglefowl • Going undercover • Drug bust • Operation Habitat • Drugs on the street • The future of drug crime

Forensics The use of forensics • The history • Securing the crime scene • Using post-mortems • Looking at the evidence: insects • Soil and seeds • Blood • DNA evidence • Bones and skulls • Clothes and shoes • Forgeries • Guns and bullets • Narcotics • Crash investigations • Explosions • Forensics and ancient history

People trafficking Defining people trafficking • History of people trafficking • The traffickers • The victims • Forced labour • The sex industry • Trafficking children • Source countries • In transit • Border controls • Case study: The European Union • Catching the criminals • Loopholes in the law • Police and welfare • Working with NGOs • Raising awareness • Taking a stand

Gun crime Defining gun crime • Which guns are used? • Who commits gun crime? • Case study: killing spree • How much gun crime is there? • Gun dealing • Gun control • Arming the police • Case study: Ganglands • Solving gun crime • Firearms in the crime lab • Case study: Washington snipers • Combating gun crime • Operation Trident • Gun crime in the media • Firearms debate

Youth crime What is youth crime? • The extent of youth crime • The causes of youth crime • Guns and knives • Case study: Columbine • Drugs and youth crime • Street gangs and crews • Case study: the Bloods and the Crips • Anti-social behaviour • Youth crime in the past • Fighting youth crime • Custodial sentences • Restorative justice • Community supervision • Young victims • Media scares • The way forward

Kidnapping and piracy Inside picture • In the past • Piracy at sea • Somalia • Case study: The MV Sirius Star • Policing the pirates • International law • Kidnapping for ransom • Abducting children • Taken hostage • Case study: Lebanon• Hijacking • Negotiation • Armed response • Case study: Flight 93 • Training and support • Surviving kidnap and piracy

Policing and justice What is criminal justice? • Rough justice • Enforcing the law • Serious crimes • Officers of the law • Case study: police racism • Guarding the guardians • Case study: Reforming the police • The Criminal Justice system • Arrest and detention • The courts • Punishment • Alternatives to prison • Youth justice • Case study: dealing with terrorism • Victims' rights • Changes to the system